50 Most Popular Classical Melodies

Arranged by David Pearl and John Nicholas

Cherry Lane Music Company
Director of Publications/Project Editor: Mark Phillips
Project Coordinator: Rebecca Skidmore

ISBN 978-1-60378-157-2

Visit our website at www.cherrylaneprint.com

Contents

Air on the G String

from Orchestral Suite No. 3

By Johann Sebastian Bach

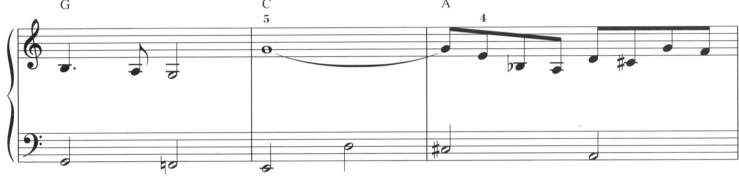

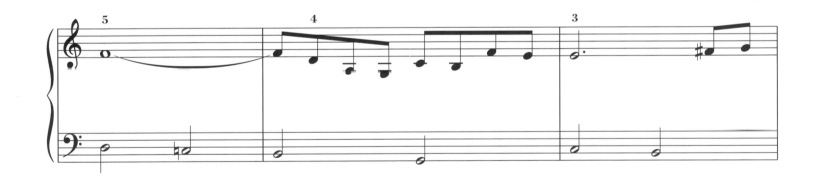

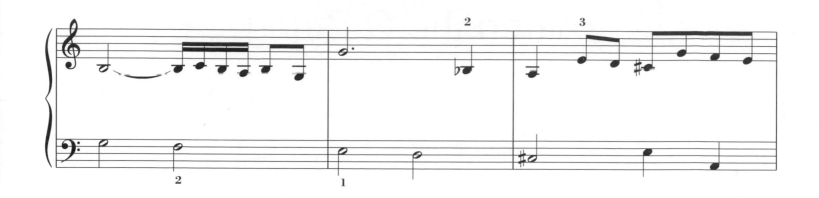

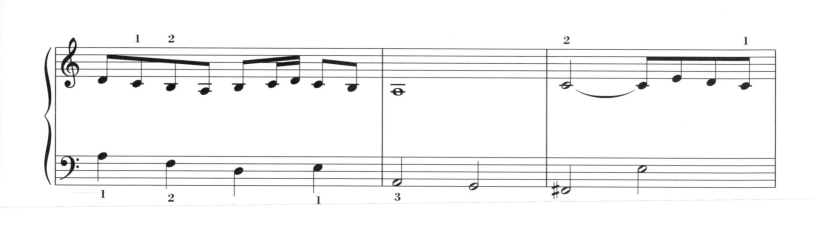

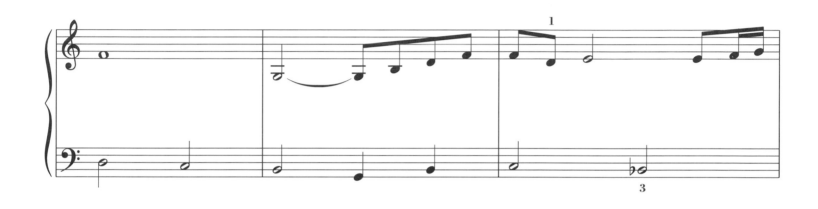

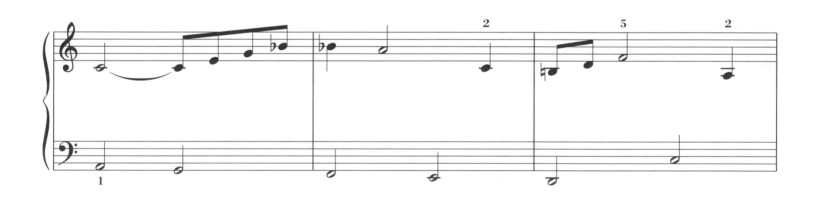

Ave Maria

By Charles Gounod
based on "Prelude in C Major" by Johann Sebastian Bach

Moderately slow

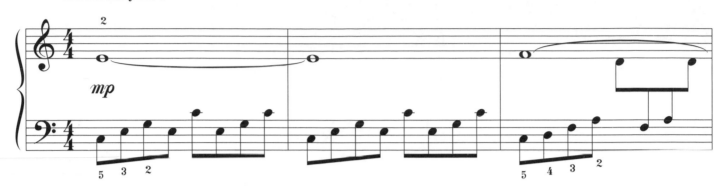

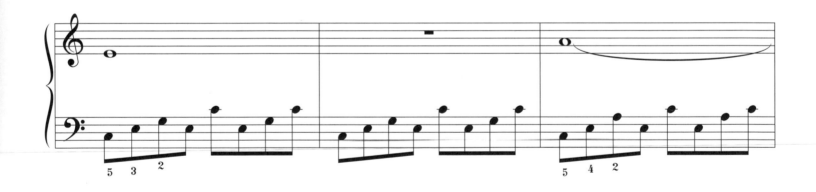

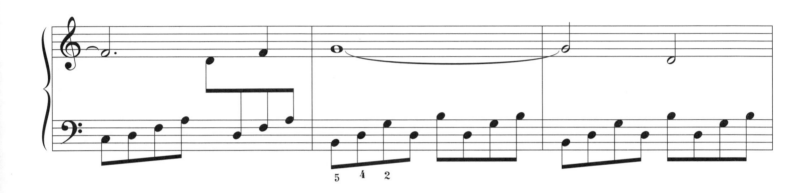

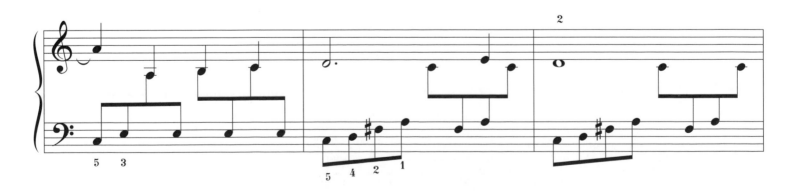

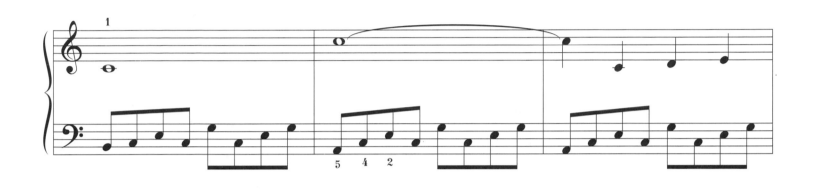

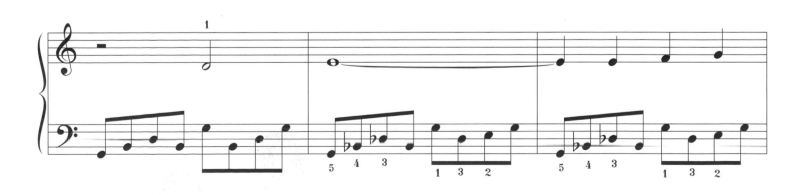

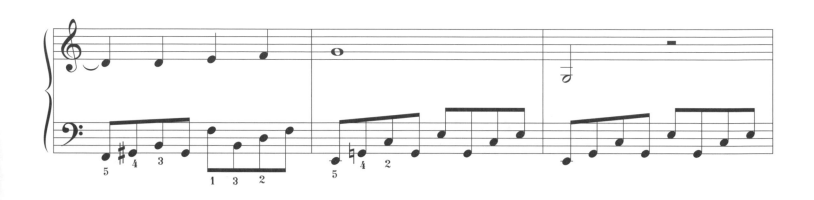

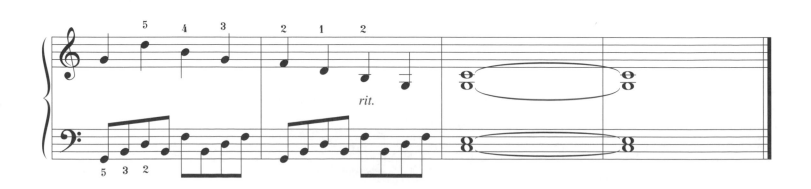

Ave Maria

By Franz Schubert

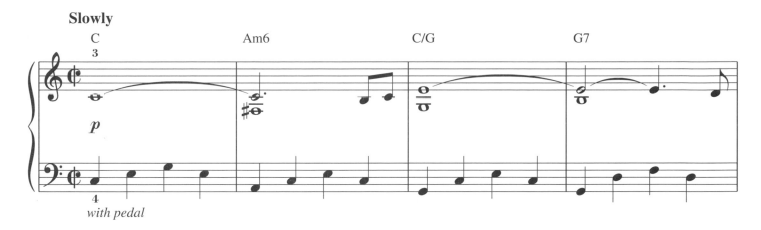

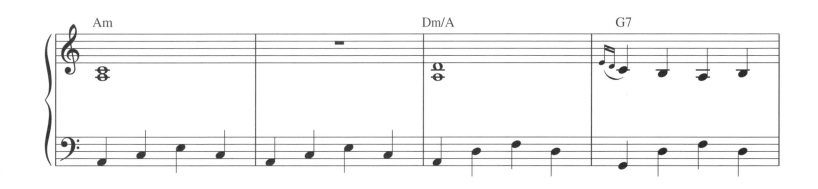

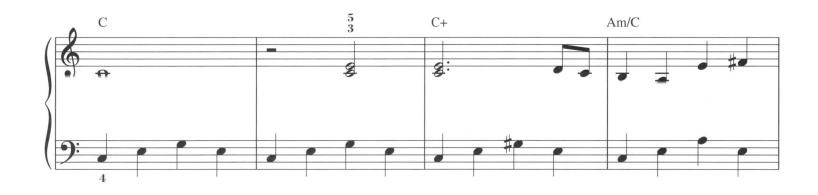

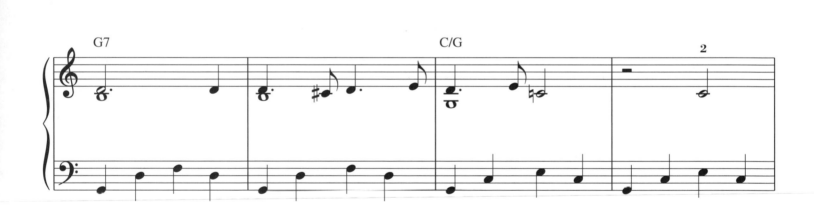

10

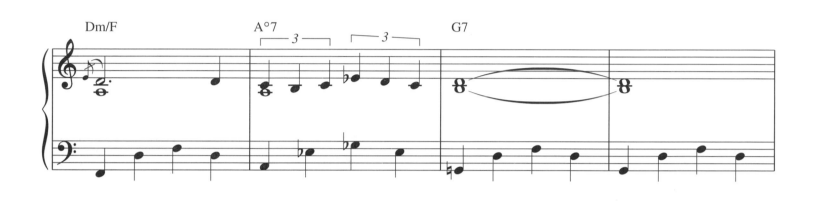

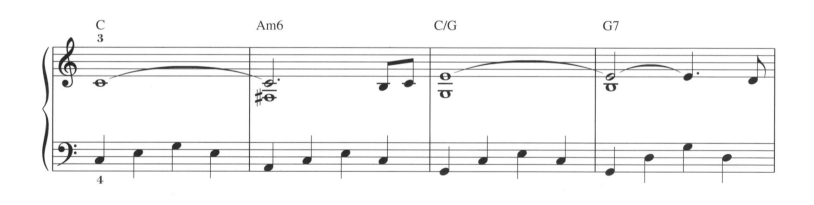

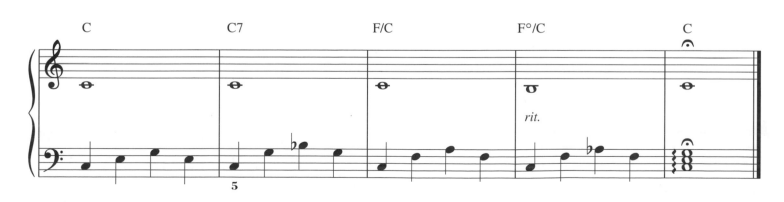

11

The Barber of Seville Overture

By Gioacchino Rossini

Barcarolle

from *Les contes d'Hoffmann*

By Jacques Offenbach

Be Thou with Me

By Johann Sebastian Bach

19

Blue Danube Waltz

By Johann Strauss, Jr.

Can Can

By Jacques Offenbach

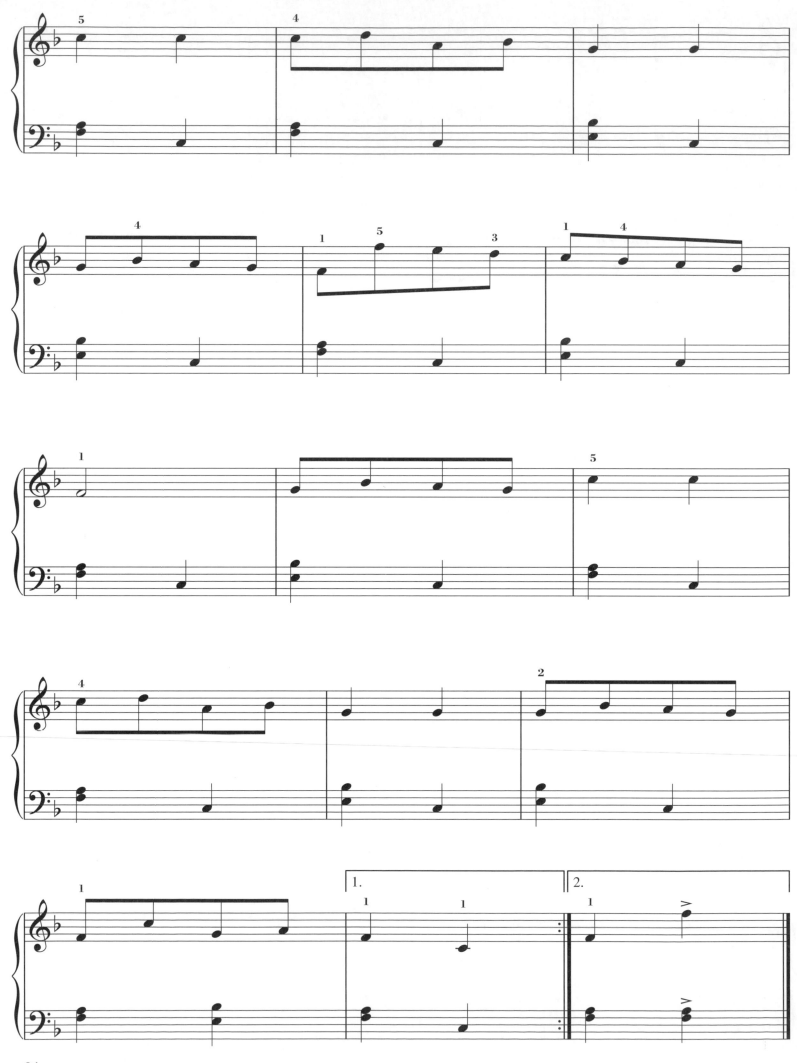

Canon in D

By Johann Pachelbel

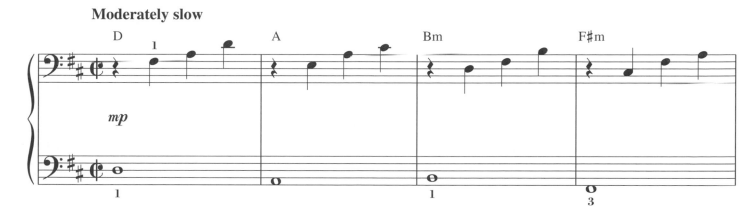

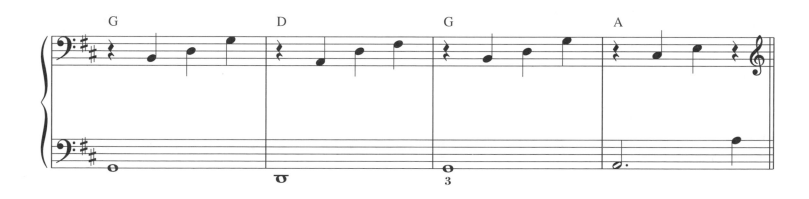

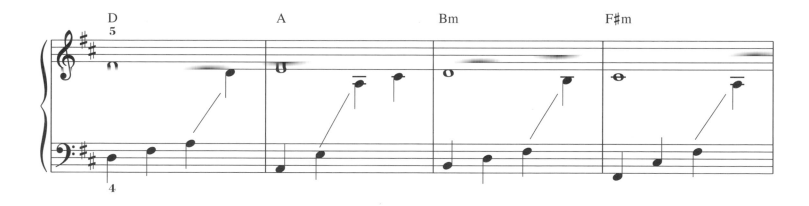

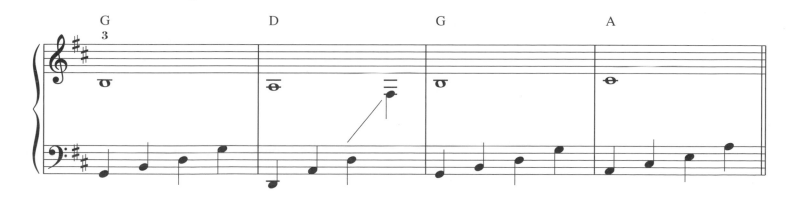

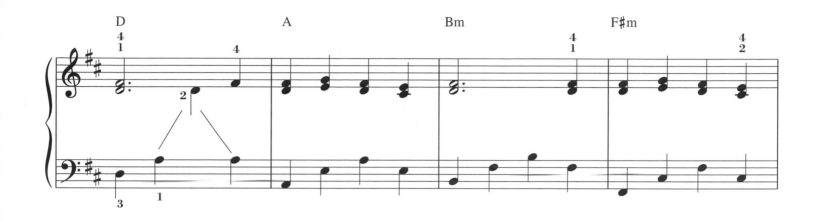

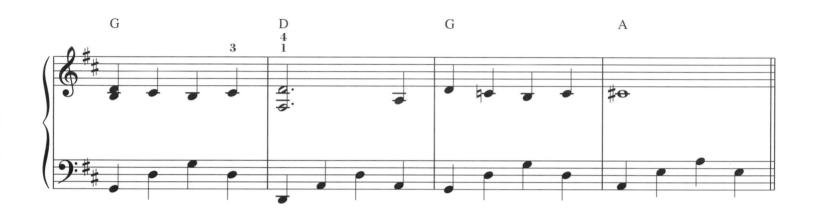

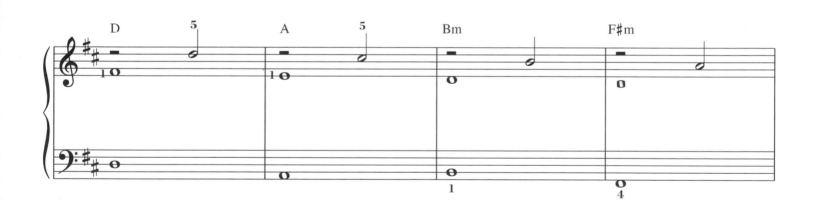

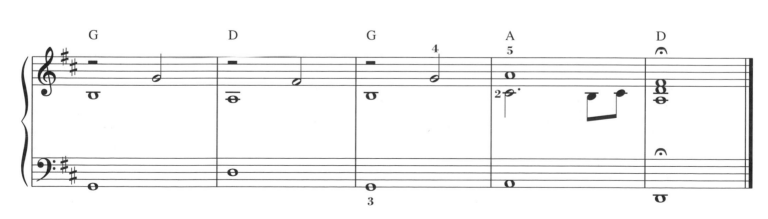

27

Cello Suite No. 1

Prelude

By Johann Sebastian Bach

Moderately slow, in 2

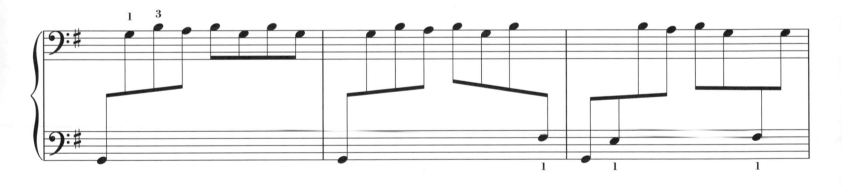

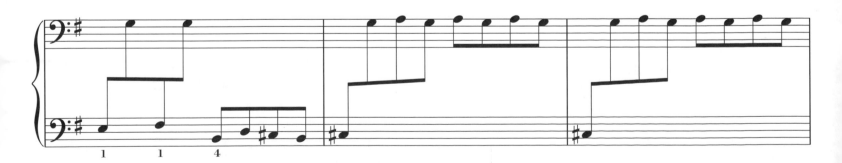

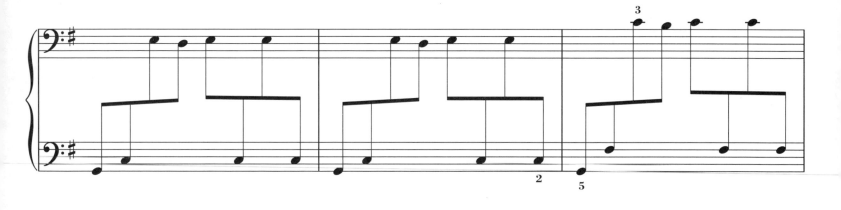

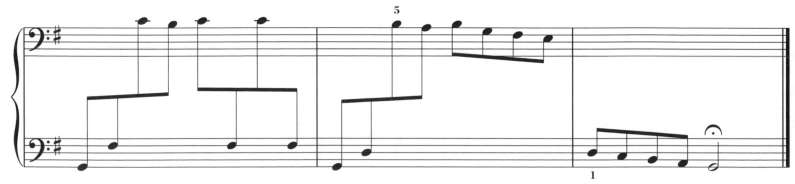

Chorale

from *St. Matthew Passion*

By Johann Sebastian Bach

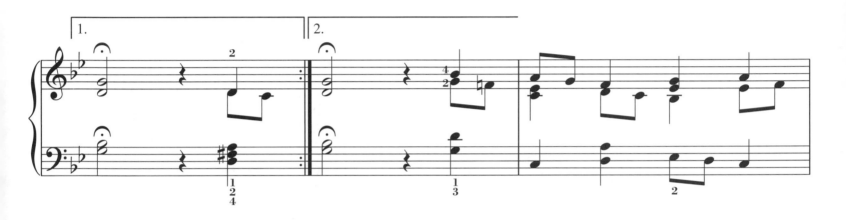

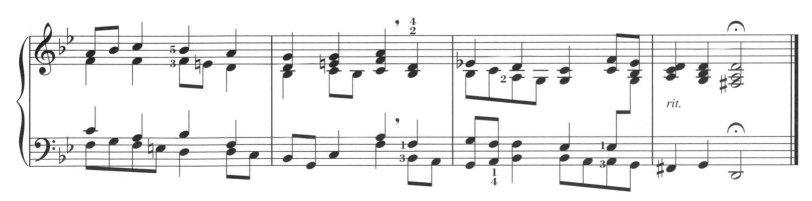

Clair de lune

By Claude Debussy

Dance of the Hours

By Amilcare Ponchielli

Dance of the Reed-Flutes

from *The Nutcracker*

By Pyotr Il'yich Tchaikovsky

Dance of the Sugar Plum Fairy

from *The Nutcracker*

By Pyotr Il'yich Tchaikovsky

To Coda

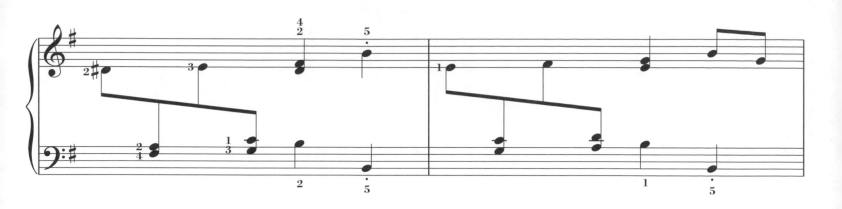

D.C. al Coda

Coda

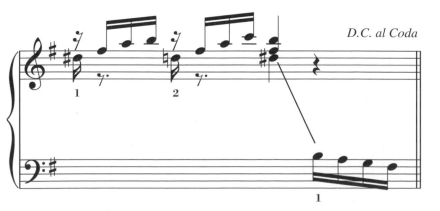

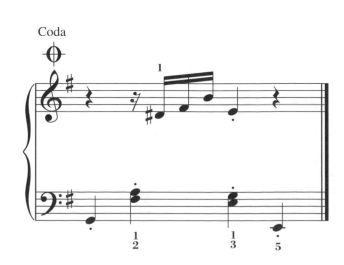

40

Eine Kleine Nachtmusik

First Movement

By Wolfgang Amadeus Mozart

Moderately fast

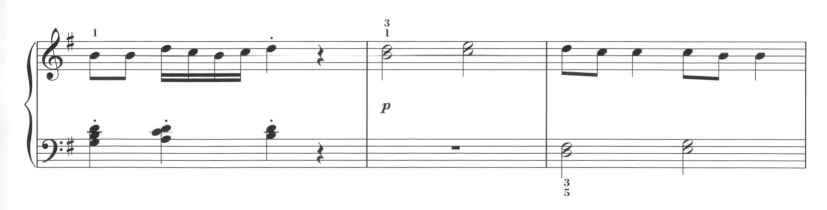

42

43

Flower Duet

from *Lakmé*

By Léo Delibes

Moderately fast

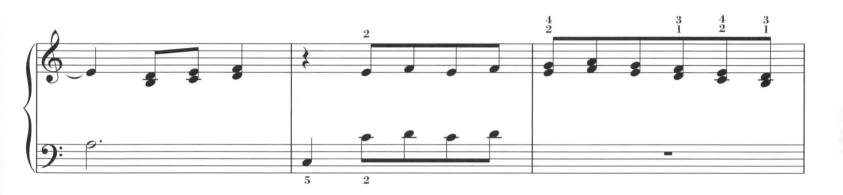

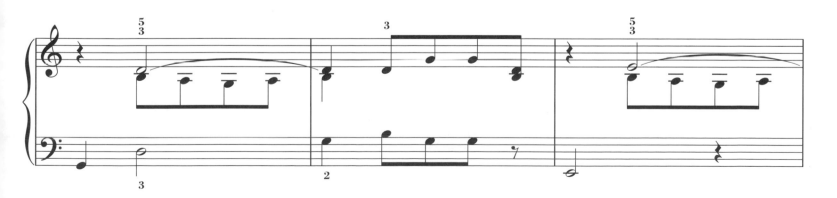

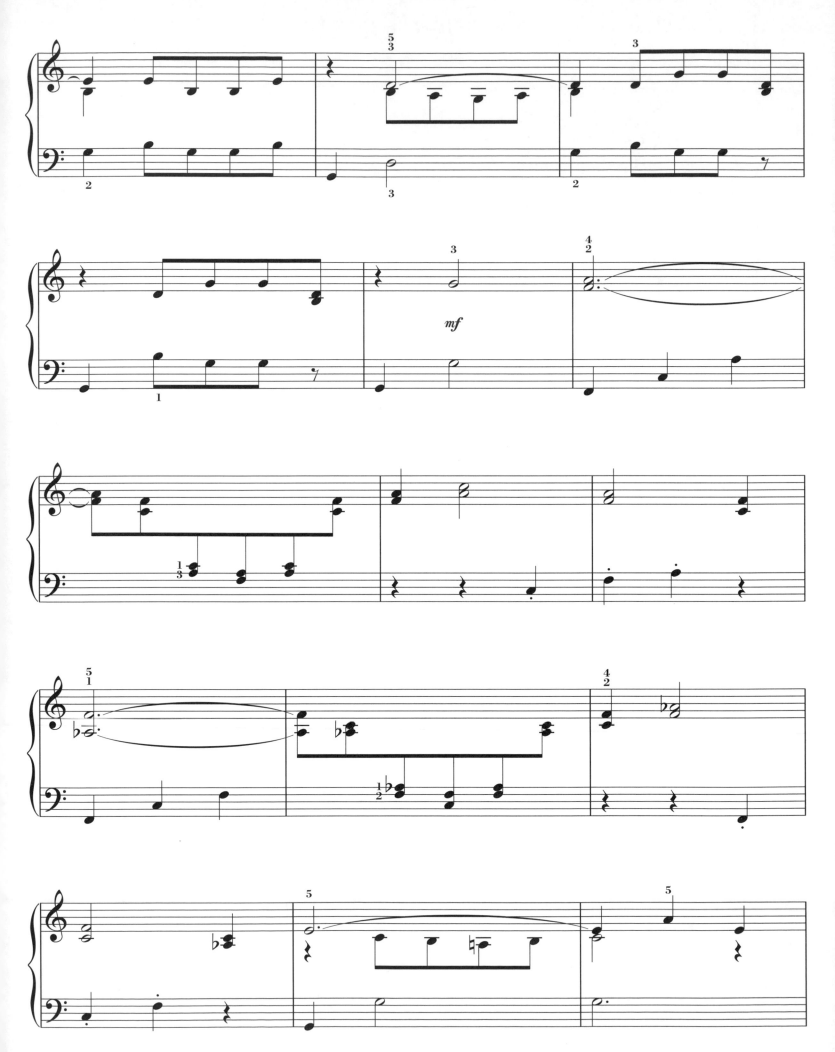

rit.

a tempo

Funeral March

from Sonata No. 2, Second Movement

By Fryderyk Chopin

Funeral March of a Marionette

By Charles Gounod

Moderately fast, in 2

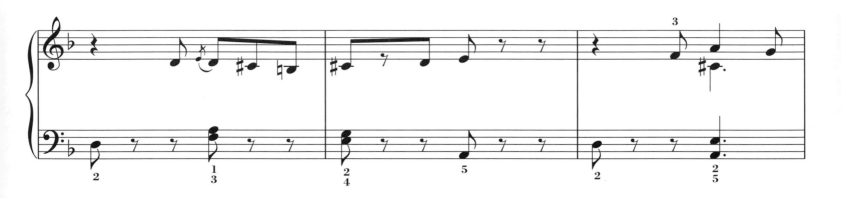

Für Elise

By Ludwig van Beethoven

Moderately

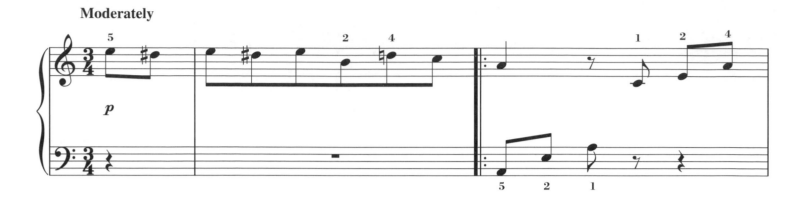

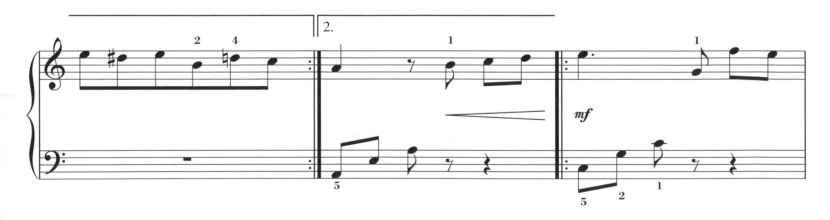

Gymnopédie No. 1

By Erik Satie

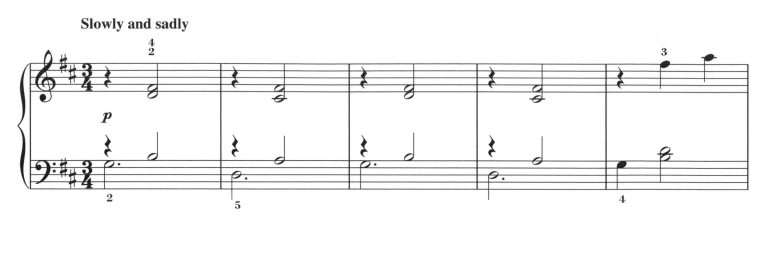

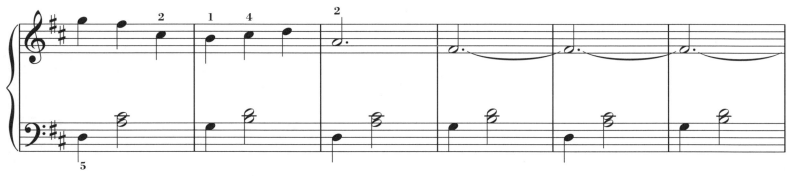

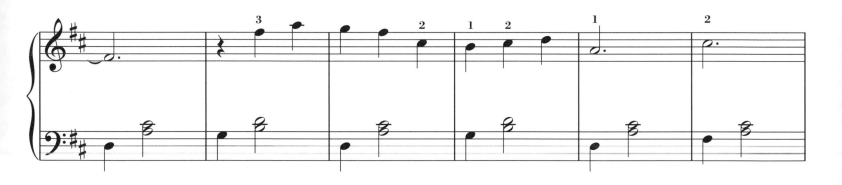

To Coda

D.C. al Coda

Coda

55

Habanera

from *Carmen*

By Georges Bizet

Hallelujah Chorus

from *The Messiah*

By George Frideric Handel

Moderately fast

Hungarian Dance No. 5

By Johannes Brahms

Slower

Tempo I

In the Hall of the Mountain King

from *Peer Gynt*

By Edvard Grieg

Jesu, Joy of Man's Desiring

By Johann Sebastian Bach

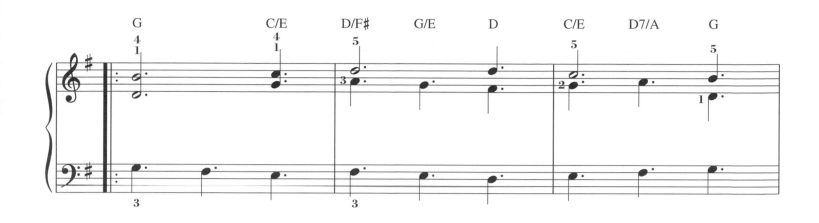

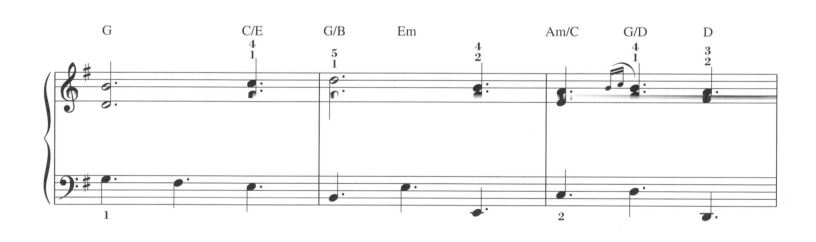

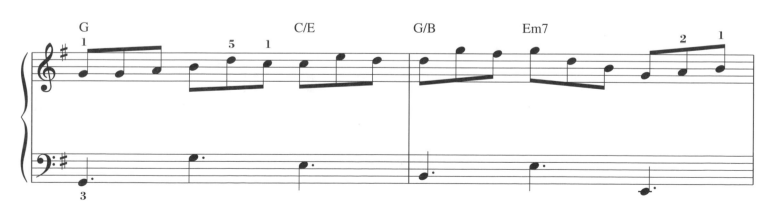

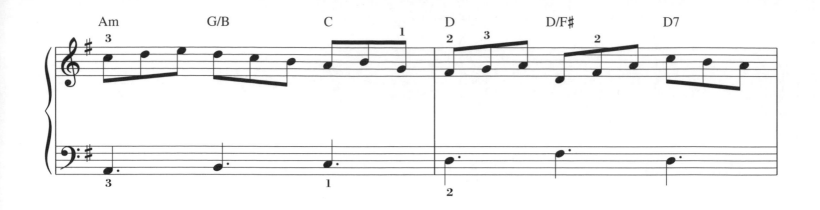

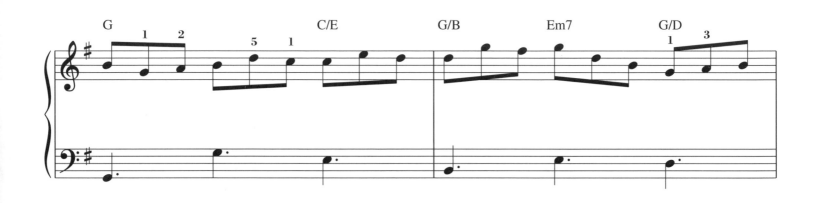

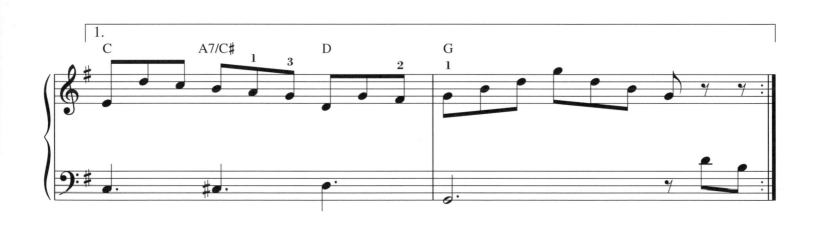

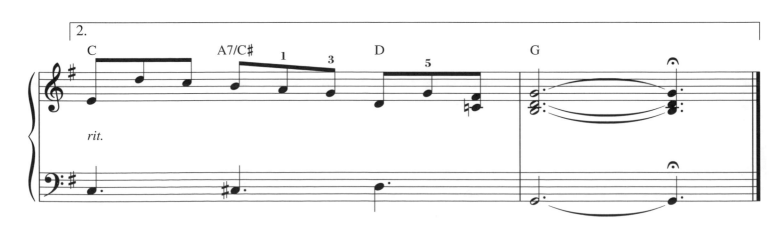

The Happy Farmer

By Robert Schumann

Love Theme from Romeo and Juliet

By Pyotr Il'yich Tchaikovsky

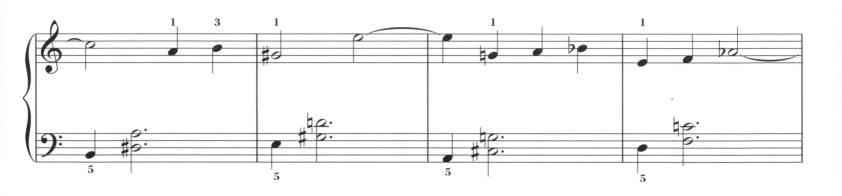

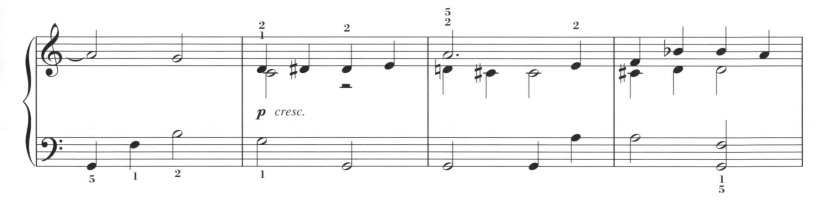

Minuet in G

by Johann Sebastian Bach

Moderately

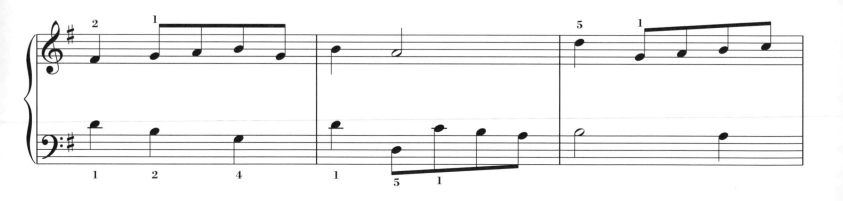

Moonlight Sonata

By Ludwig van Beethoven

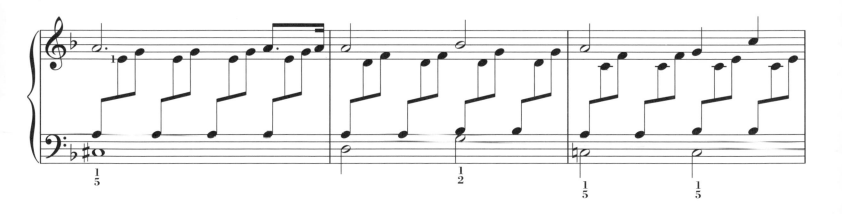

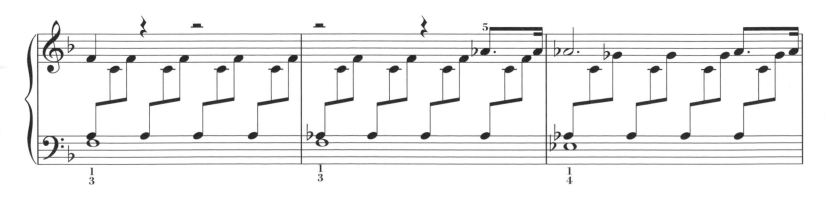

75

Morning

from *Peer Gynt*

By Edvard Grieg

Moderately slow

Piano Concerto No. 2
Second Movement

By Sergei Rachmaninoff

Slowly

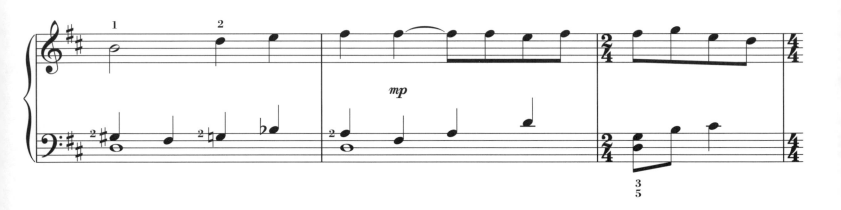

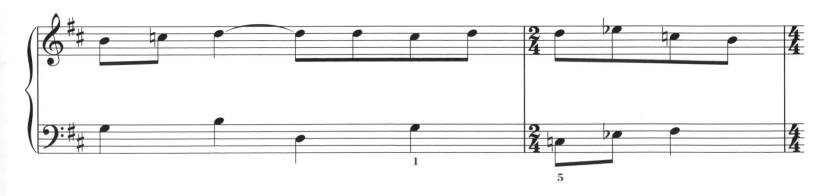

79

Pictures at an Exhibition

Promenade

By Modest Mussorgsky

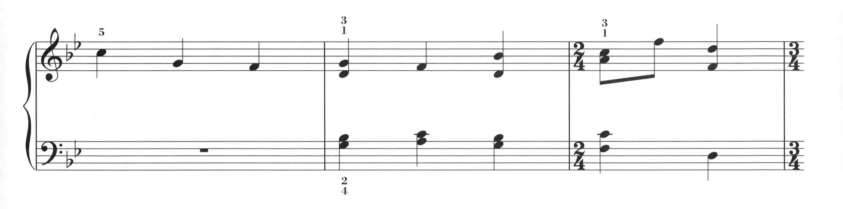

Lullaby

By Johannes Brahms

Polovetsian Dance

By Alexander Borodin

Pomp and Circumstance

Music by Edward Elgar

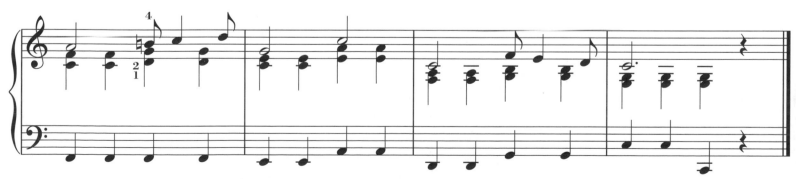

Rhapsody on a Theme by Paganini

By Sergei Rachmaninoff

The Skaters Waltz

By Emil Waldteufel

Medium Waltz

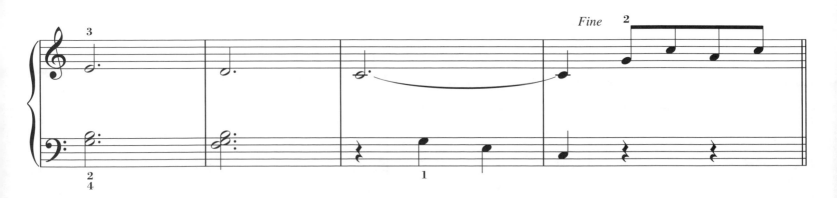

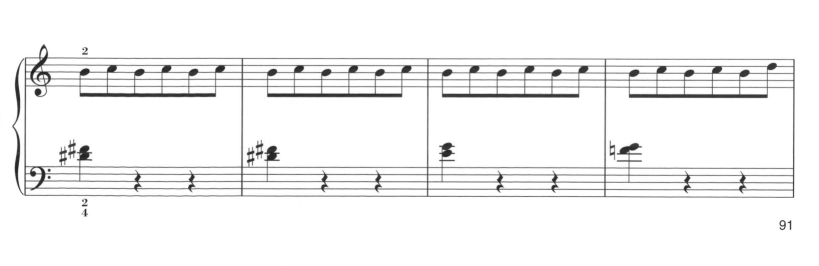

D.C. al Fine

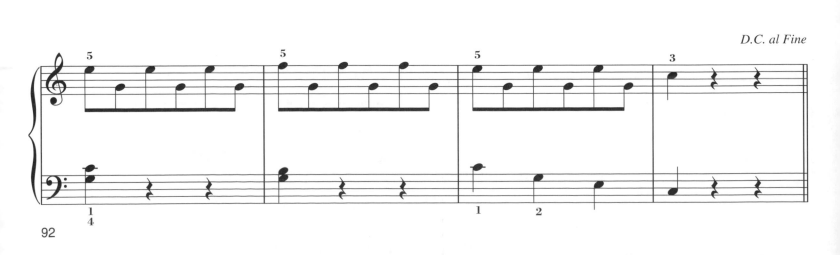

92

Symphony No. 40

First Movement

By Wolfgang Amadeus Mozart

Moderately, in 2

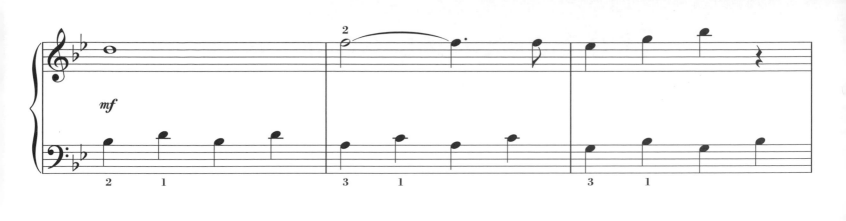

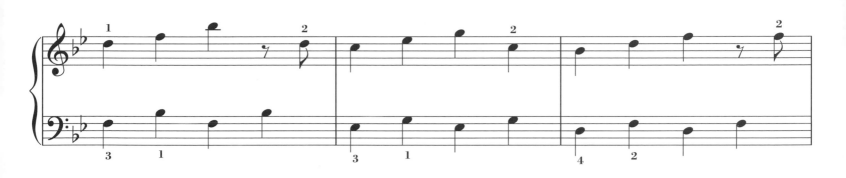

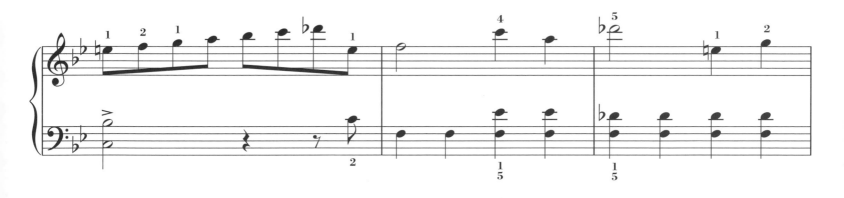

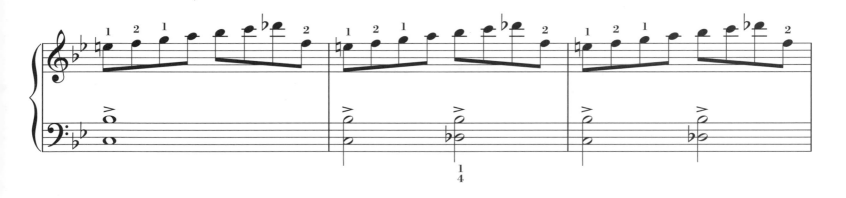

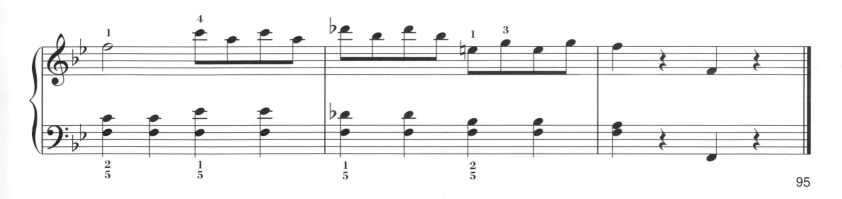

The Sorcerer's Apprentice

By Paul Dukas

97

Surprise Symphony

By Franz Joseph Haydn

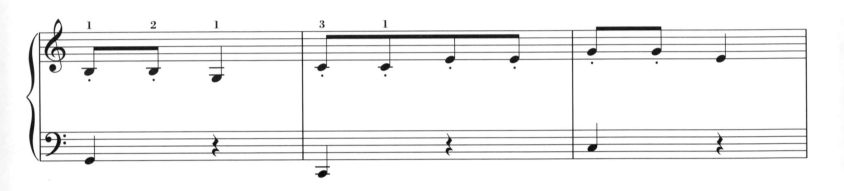

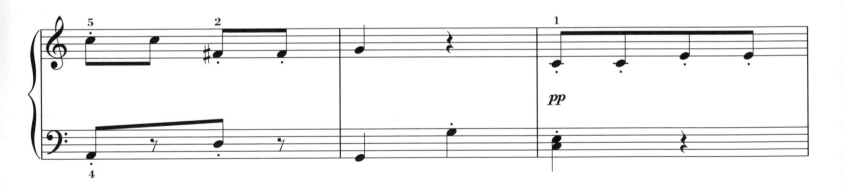

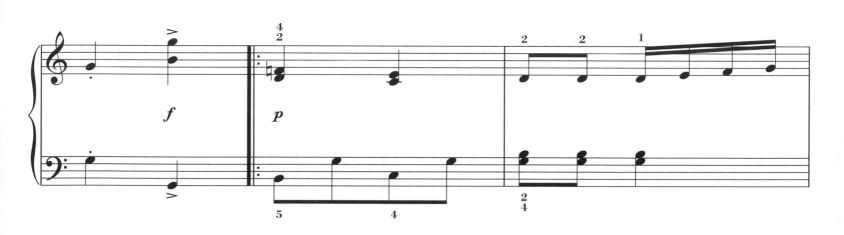

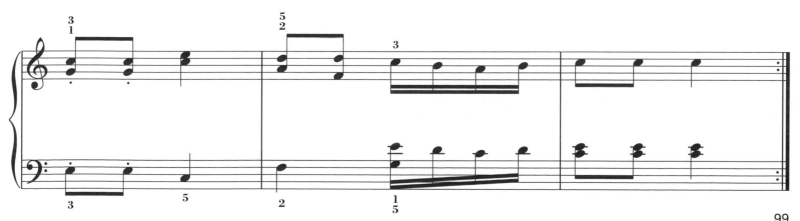

The Swan

from *Carnival of the Animals*

By Camille Saint-Saëns
(1835–1921)

Slowly

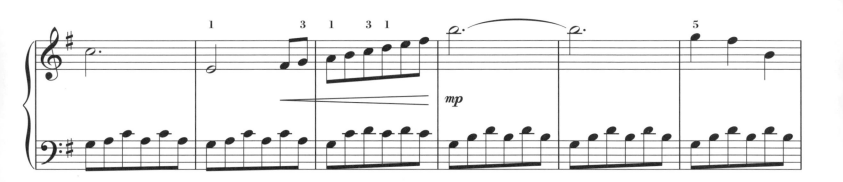

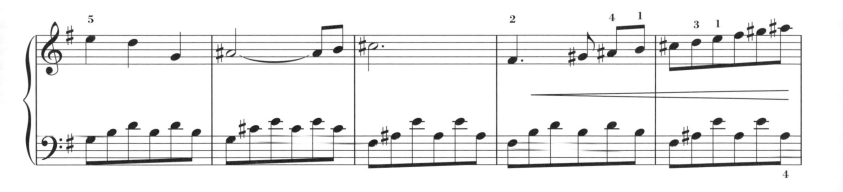

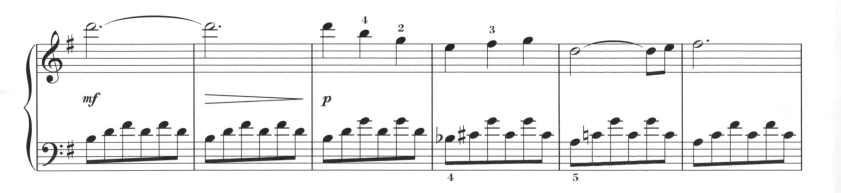

Swan Lake

Waltz

By Pyotr Il'yich Tchaikovsky

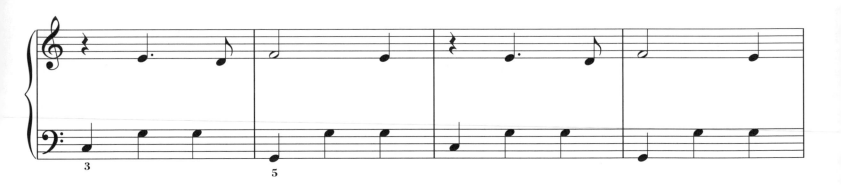

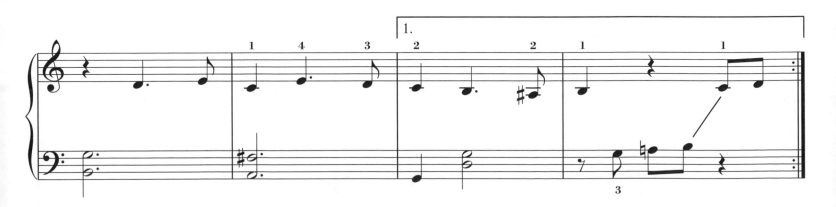

Symphony No. 1

Fourth Movement

By Johannes Brahms

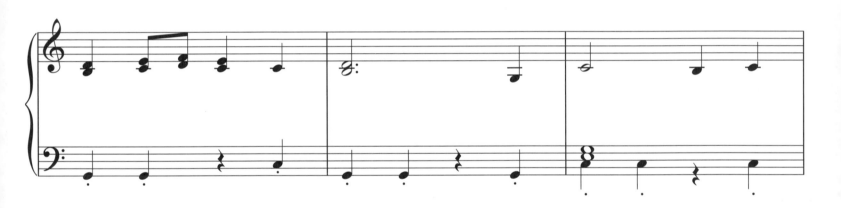

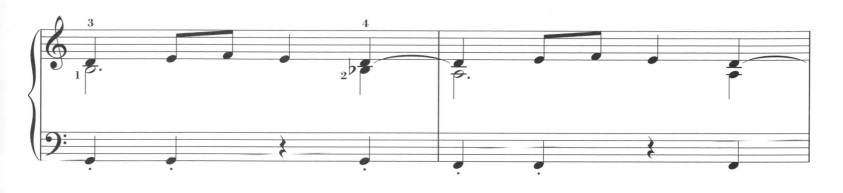

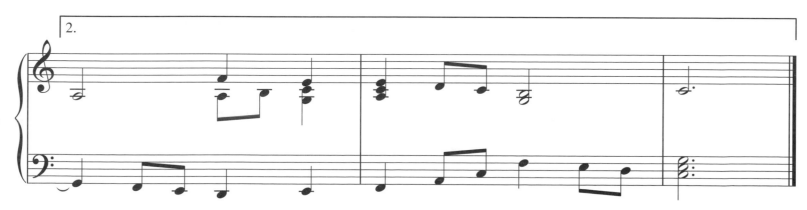

Symphony No. 3
Third Movement

By Johannes Brahms

Symphony No. 5

First Movement

By Ludwig van Beethoven

Moderately fast

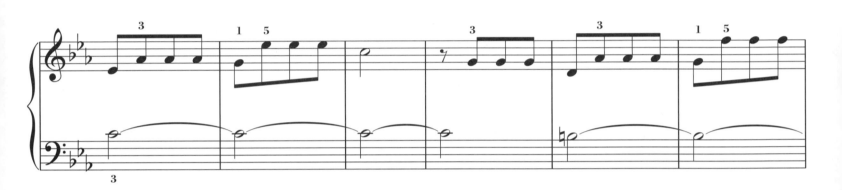

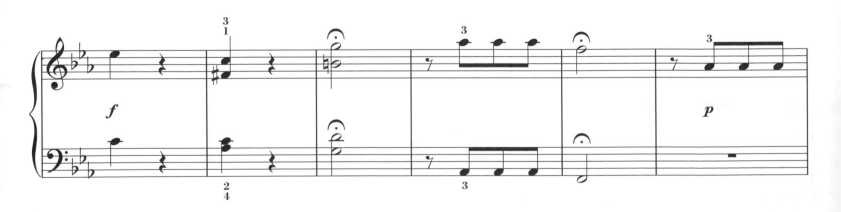

111

Symphony No. 9

"Ode to Joy"

By Ludwig van Beethoven

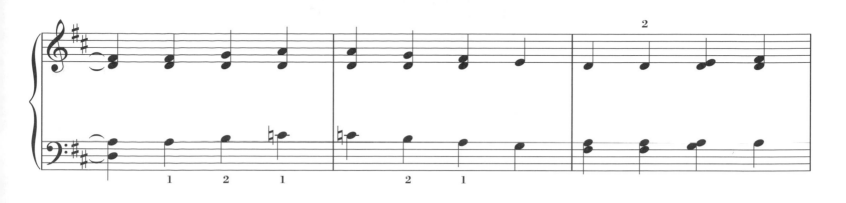

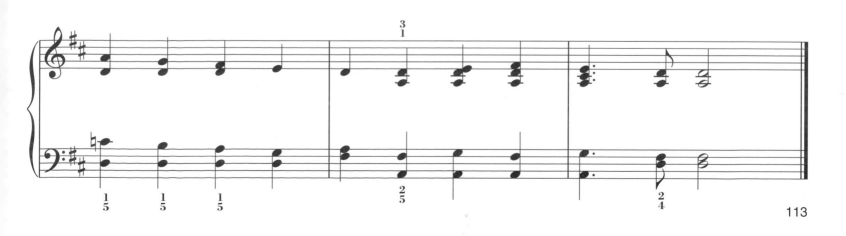

Toreador Song

from *Carmen*

By Goerges Bizet

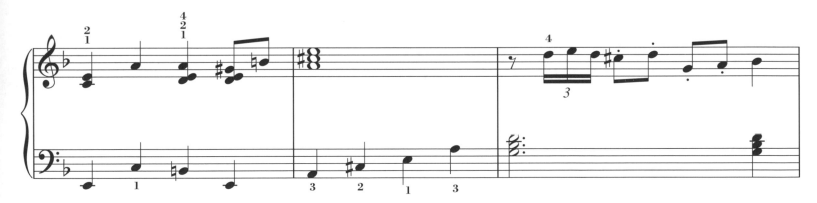

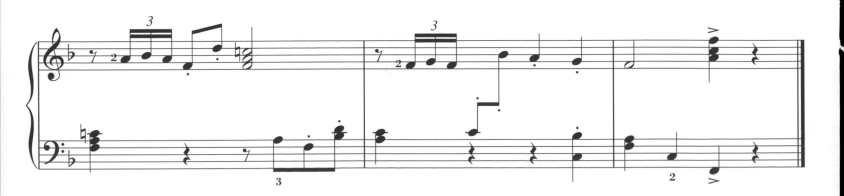

Waltz of the Flowers

from *The Nutcracker*

By Pyotr Il'yich Tchaikovsky

Moderately slow, in 1

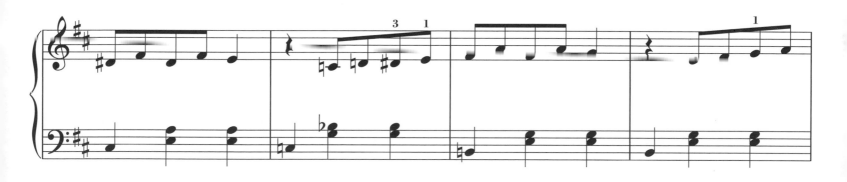

116

William Tell Overture

By Gioacchino Rossini